BEHIND THE WHEEL™

Kevin Harvick

NASCAR Driver

Greg Roza

rosen publishing's
rosen central®

New York

Published in 2009 by The Rosen Publishing Group, Inc.
29 East 21st Street, New York, NY 10010

Library of Congress Cataloging-in-Publication Data

Roza, Greg.
Kevin Harvick: NASCAR driver / Greg Roza.—1st ed.
    p. cm.—(Behind the wheel)
Includes bibliographical references and index.
ISBN-13: 978-1-4042-1899-4 (library binding)
ISBN-13: 978-1-4358-5406-2 (pbk)
ISBN-13: 978-1-4358-5412-3 (6 pack)
1. Harvick, Kevin—Juvenile literature. 2. Automobile racing drivers—
United States—Biography. I. Title.
GV1032.H36R69 2009
796.72092—dc22
[B]
                                                            2008022088

Manufactured in the United States of America

On the cover: Kevin Harvick helps prepare his #29 car for the 2004
Subway 400 in Rockingham, North Carolina.

CONTENTS

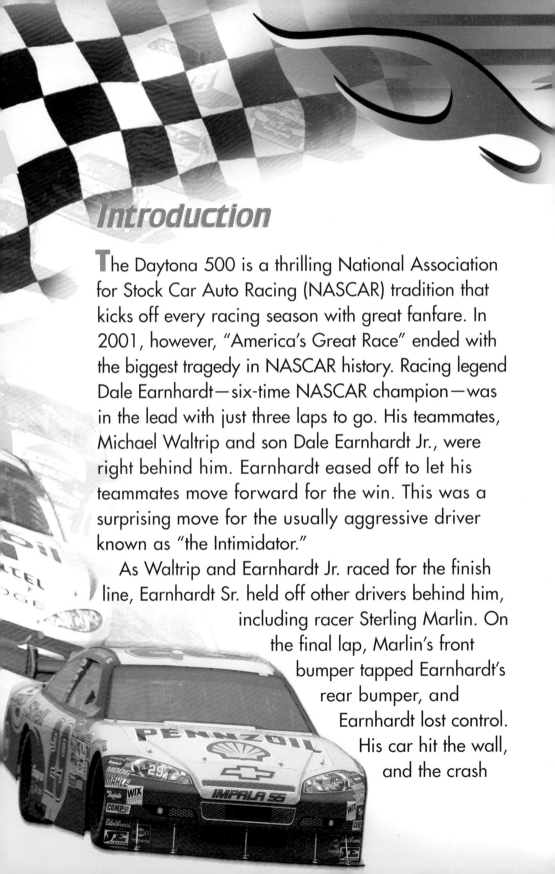

Introduction

The Daytona 500 is a thrilling National Association for Stock Car Auto Racing (NASCAR) tradition that kicks off every racing season with great fanfare. In 2001, however, "America's Great Race" ended with the biggest tragedy in NASCAR history. Racing legend Dale Earnhardt—six-time NASCAR champion—was in the lead with just three laps to go. His teammates, Michael Waltrip and son Dale Earnhardt Jr., were right behind him. Earnhardt eased off to let his teammates move forward for the win. This was a surprising move for the usually aggressive driver known as "the Intimidator."

As Waltrip and Earnhardt Jr. raced for the finish line, Earnhardt Sr. held off other drivers behind him, including racer Sterling Marlin. On the final lap, Marlin's front bumper tapped Earnhardt's rear bumper, and Earnhardt lost control. His car hit the wall, and the crash killed him instantly. His teammates won the race, but they and the rest of the racing world were horrified to hear of the passing of a racing legend.

The owner of Earnhardt's team, Richard Childress, had to find a replacement driver for the rest of the 2001 season. Childress asked up-and-comer Kevin Harvick to step in and race in the Winston Cup Series (later called the Nextel Cup Series and now known as the Sprint Cup Series). Harvick was a Busch Series (today called the Nationwide Series) driver for Childress's team, and he had won Rookie of the Year honors in 2000. Now, in just his second season, Childress was asking Harvick to race full-time in both the Busch Series and the Winston Cup Series. (The Winston/Sprint Cup is NASCAR's top level of competition in which America's best stock car racers compete. The Busch/Nationwide Cup is NASCAR's second-highest level of stock car racing. Nationwide cars are similar to, but less powerful than, the cars raced at NASCAR's top level. The prize money is less and the racing season is shorter than that of the Sprint Cup Series). Racing full time in two NASCAR series was something no other driver had done before Harvick did it. It would have been a difficult feat for most racers. But also having to fill the shoes of perhaps the greatest driver of all time was another story altogether.

Harvick is no ordinary driver, however. Many people in NASCAR, including Childress, knew he had the same determined, reckless style as the man he was replacing.

A smiling Kevin Harvick salutes fans before a 2001 NASCAR race. Harvick's charming smile has become a familiar sight on race day.

Harvick did not disappoint, and 2001 would prove to be a high point in the young driver's career. In just his third start, Harvick won his first Winston Cup race. He finished the year with a Busch Series championship and Rookie of the Year honors in the Winston Cup Series. Despite the tragic start to the 2001 season, Harvick and Richard Childress Racing had made NASCAR history.

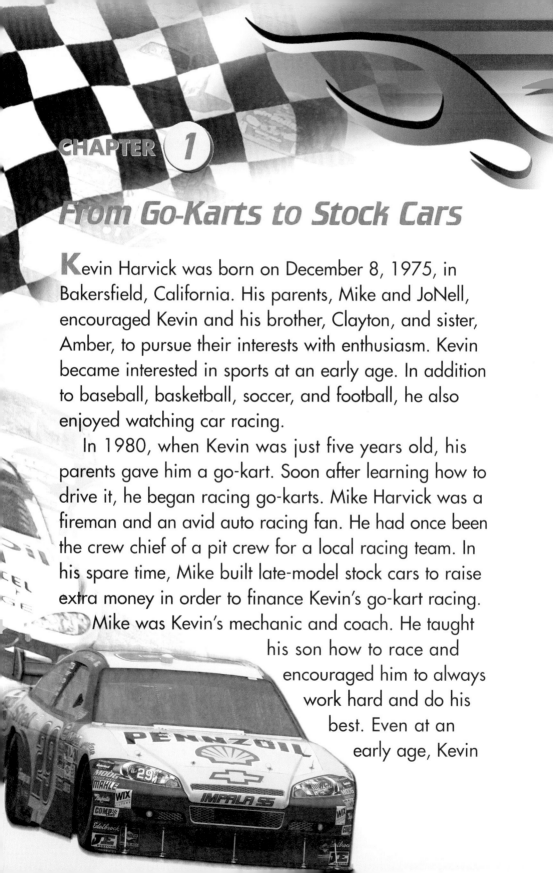

CHAPTER 1

From Go-Karts to Stock Cars

Kevin Harvick was born on December 8, 1975, in Bakersfield, California. His parents, Mike and JoNell, encouraged Kevin and his brother, Clayton, and sister, Amber, to pursue their interests with enthusiasm. Kevin became interested in sports at an early age. In addition to baseball, basketball, soccer, and football, he also enjoyed watching car racing.

In 1980, when Kevin was just five years old, his parents gave him a go-kart. Soon after learning how to drive it, he began racing go-karts. Mike Harvick was a fireman and an avid auto racing fan. He had once been the crew chief of a pit crew for a local racing team. In his spare time, Mike built late-model stock cars to raise extra money in order to finance Kevin's go-kart racing. Mike was Kevin's mechanic and coach. He taught his son how to race and encouraged him to always work hard and do his best. Even at an early age, Kevin was very competitive. He was known to push his way to the head of the pack by any means necessary, and many other racers considered him dangerous. But Kevin was just doing what his father had taught him. Mike's tutelage paid off. By the time Kevin was 14, he had won seven national go-kart championships and two grand national championships.

Starting Young

In 1991, when Kevin was just 15, his father built him his first stock car. In 1992, he began racing in the NASCAR AutoZone Elite Southwest Series. In 1993, Kevin took first place at the Mesa Marin Raceway in his hometown of Bakersfield. He accomplished this while still attending high school!

When Kevin graduated high school in 1995, he began racing in the NASCAR Featherlite Southwest Series. NASCAR Featherlite (now called the Whelen Modified Tour) is NASCAR's oldest modified division and the only open-wheeled division (meaning the wheels are not covered by the body of the car). Kevin immediately made a name for himself as a rising star. He had one first place finish that year and finished in 11th place overall, earning the Rookie of the Year Award. Kevin had enrolled in Bakersfield Junior College while making progress as a driver. However, he soon realized that he was destined to be a NASCAR driver.

A Solid Start

In addition to the Featherlite division, Harvick began racing in Winston West (today called the NASCAR Camping World West Series) and Craftsman Truck races (NASCAR's modified truck racing series). He continued to race with a pedal-to-the-metal personality.

Harvick lines up in his #75 Chevy truck for the start of the 1998 Kroger 225 Craftsman Truck Series race in Louisville, Kentucky. He started in second place and finished in 13th.

This driving style angered veteran racers, but it also allowed him to succeed in NASCAR at an early age.

Halfway through the 1997 season, Harvick became a member of Spears Motorsports, owned by Wayne and Connie Spears. In 1998, he completed his first full season racing in both the Craftsman Truck Series and the Camping World West Series. After winning five Camping World West races, Harvick was crowned champion of that division. He came in 17th in the Craftsman Truck Series. He wanted to do better in 1999.

Harvick entered 25 Craftsman races in 1999 and finished in the top ten 11 times. He finished the season in 12th place and made $300,000. That year he also entered two Automobile Racing Club of America (ARCA) races, earning second and third place finishes. On October 23, 1999, Harvick appeared in his first Nationwide Series race—the Kmart 400 held at the North Carolina Motor Speedway in Rockingham, North Carolina. He drove the #65 Chevrolet and qualified in 24th place. However, he experienced an engine failure and wasn't able to finish the race. Despite the poor showing, Harvick's career was about to take a turn for the better.

Taking Notice

By the end of the 1999 season, Harvick had gained a reputation as a hard-racing, straight-talking driver. People were starting to take notice of the up-and-comer. Richard

Harvick relaxes on his truck before the GoRacing 200 at the Michigan International Speedway on July 24, 1999.

Childress is a retired NASCAR driver and successful car owner. Together, Childress and legendary driver Dale Earnhardt won a total of six NASCAR Winston Cup championships in one of the racing world's most successful owner-driver partnerships. Childress knew Harvick had a future in NASCAR, and he wanted to be the one to give him his start as a full-time driver.

At the end of the 1999 racing season, Harvick was signed to Richard Childress Racing to compete in the Busch Series full time. The Busch Series (today called the Nationwide Series) is similar to minor league baseball. It is a training ground for drivers as they prepare for the "major leagues"—the Sprint Cup Series (formerly the Winston Cup Series). Harvick would be driving the #2

AC Delco–sponsored Chevrolet. He drove the car so hard in practice that he blew a tire two times. This could have resulted in tragedy for such an inexperienced driver, but Harvick handled the mishaps well, proving he was up to the challenge.

It took Harvick very little time to grow accustomed to competition in the Busch Series. He scored three top-ten finishes in the first ten races. In May, he finished third at the Hardee's 250 in Richmond, Virginia. Soon after this race, Harvick came in second at the Myrtle Beach 250 in South Carolina. Many NASCAR fans and experts were expecting him to win his first Busch Series race in the very near future.

Harvick's First Busch Series Victory

The Carquest Auto Parts 250 was held at the Gateway International Raceway in Madison, Illinois, on July 29, 2000. For the first half of the race, Harvick battled for first place, sometimes leading the pack for several laps at a time. On lap 166, he took the lead for good. Not only did he win the race, but he also set a record for the event with an average speed of 116.595 miles per hour (187 kilometers per hour). The win lifted him into fourth place in the Busch Cup standings.

By the end of the 2000 season, Harvick had notched three wins and finished third in points. In addition to the

LIST OF AWARDS

Seven national go-kart championships
Two grand national go-kart championships
1995 NASCAR Featherlite Southwest Series Rookie of the Year
1998 NASCAR Winston West Series champion
2000 NASCAR Busch Series Rookie of the Year
2001 Busch Series champion
2001 NASCAR Winston Cup Rookie of the Year
2002 IROC champion
2003 Brickyard 400 winner
2006 Busch Series champion
2007 Daytona 500 winner
2007 Nextel All-Star Challenge winner

win in Madison, Harvick also came in first in the Food City 250 at the Bristol Motor Speedway in Tennessee and was victorious in Sam's Town 250 at the Memphis Motorsports Park. At the end of the season, his 4,113 points and $995,274 in earnings tied the record for most wins and highest finish by a Busch Series rookie. Having earned the nickname "Happy" due to his constant smile, Harvick was the unanimous choice for Busch Series Rookie of the Year. This truly gave him something to smile about.

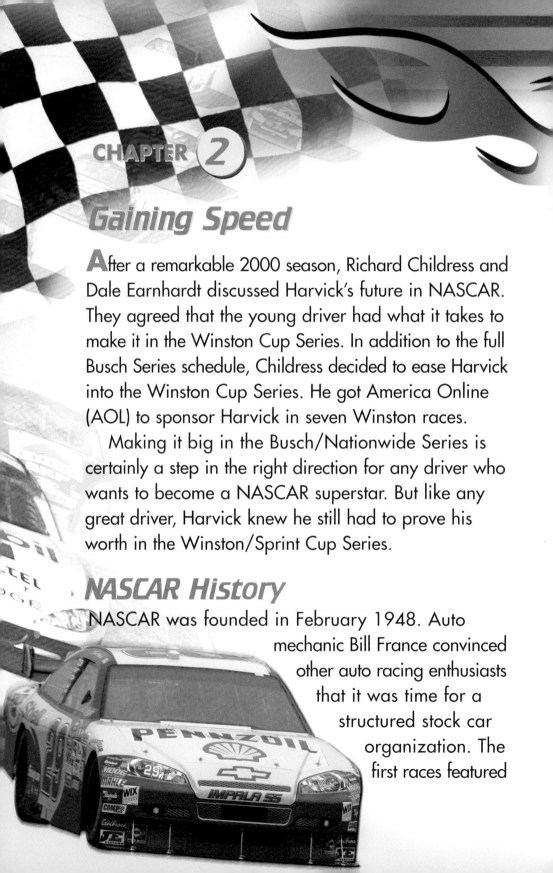

CHAPTER 2

Gaining Speed

After a remarkable 2000 season, Richard Childress and Dale Earnhardt discussed Harvick's future in NASCAR. They agreed that the young driver had what it takes to make it in the Winston Cup Series. In addition to the full Busch Series schedule, Childress decided to ease Harvick into the Winston Cup Series. He got America Online (AOL) to sponsor Harvick in seven Winston races.

Making it big in the Busch/Nationwide Series is certainly a step in the right direction for any driver who wants to become a NASCAR superstar. But like any great driver, Harvick knew he still had to prove his worth in the Winston/Sprint Cup Series.

NASCAR History

NASCAR was founded in February 1948. Auto mechanic Bill France convinced other auto racing enthusiasts that it was time for a structured stock car organization. The first races featured

On February 22, 1959, Bob Welborn (#3 car) passed Glenn "Fireball" Roberts to move into first place during a qualifying heat for the first ever Daytona 500.

modified cars, meaning that mechanics had made significant changes to ordinary automobiles after they had come off the assembly line. The first "strictly stock" race was held in June 1949 in Charlotte, North Carolina. It was an immediate popular sensation. About 13,000 people came to watch the race.

The new sport quickly grew in popularity. In 1959, the first race was held at the legendary Daytona International Speedway in Daytona, Florida. The 2.5-mile (4 km) banked-turn track was an amazing sight for fans and drivers. It replaced the previous track in Daytona, which was a 4.8-mile (7.7 km) track consisting of a stretch of

Atlantic coast highway and an equal stretch of shore. Soon after, taped NASCAR races were shown on television, and the fan base grew quickly.

The modern era of NASCAR began in the early 1970s. The tobacco company R. J. Reynolds began financing the sport, which helped it to grow. The pro series took on the name the Winston Cup. More and more previously recorded races were shown on television, although the first live NASCAR event was not televised until 1979. This increased exposure led to an explosion in advertising as companies realized the financial benefits of being associated in the public's mind with NASCAR. Over the next 30 years, constant innovation to track and car technology, as well as improved safety, made NASCAR America's most popular spectator sport.

NASCAR Series

The Sprint Cup Series is the top division in NASCAR. The terms "NASCAR" and "Cup" are generally used to refer to this series. It is the series that all drivers hope to compete in one day.

The Nationwide Cup Series is a training ground for young drivers hoping to make it to the Sprint Series. Many Sprint Series drivers also race in Nationwide Series races, which often occur at the same tracks the day before Sprint Series races. This is a trend Kevin Harvick started in 2001.

Craftsman Truck races are just as exciting as Sprint and Nationwide Cup races. In this photo, driver Stacy Compton (#86 truck) prepares to cross the finish line at a race in Topeka, Kansas.

The Craftsman Truck Series is the third national NASCAR series. It features modified pickup trucks. Created in 1995, this series was originally considered an exhibition series. It soon took on a reputation as a "seniors" circuit. Today, however, it is more similar to the Nationwide Series. Some drivers even go from the Craftsman Truck Series to the Sprint Series without ever racing in the Nationwide Series.

In addition to these three national series, NASCAR sanctions several regional and semiprofessional racing series. It is in these smaller divisions that most drivers get their start. Many tracks across the United States run races under the title Whelen All-American Series, which is split into four divisions. The Whelen Modified Tour features cars with open wheels and has a Northern and Southern division. The Camping World Series has an Eastern and a Western division and features cars similar to, but less powerful than, those raced in the Nationwide Series. NASCAR also sanctions two international divisions, the Canadian Tire Series in Canada and the Corona Series in Mexico.

Filling in for a Legend

Harvick had big hopes for the Busch Series. Earning Rookie of the Year honors was a great start, but he had his sights set on the 2001 Busch Cup championship. However, Harvick's plans for the season took a drastic turn when Winston Cup racer Dale Earnhardt died during the 2001 Daytona 500. The racing world was stunned and saddened by the loss of a NASCAR legend. Once the initial shock wore off, however, Richard Childress realized that he needed to find a full-time driver to fill in for Earnhardt. He immediately thought of Harvick.

After the Richard Childress Racing team discussed the move, Harvick agreed to race in the Winston Cup Series full time. However, he refused to abandon his Busch Series team. He believed that he had worked too hard and that they were about to have a groundbreaking season, and he didn't want to throw that away. So, Harvick suggested something that had never been done before—racing full time in both the Busch and Winston series.

NASCAR POINTS SYSTEM

NASCAR race winners receive 185 points. Second-place finishers receive 170 points. Drivers three through six receive 5 fewer points than the driver who finished ahead of them. Drivers seven through eleven receive 4 fewer points than the driver who finished ahead of them. Drivers who finish in 12th place or lower receive 3 points fewer than the driver who finished ahead of them. The last driver, who comes in 43rd place, receives 34 points. Drivers also earn 5 points if they led the race for at least one lap. The driver that led the race for the most laps receives an additional 10 points.

Car owners earn points in a similar manner. However, owners earn points even if their driver fails to qualify for the race. The fastest non-qualifier for the race earns 31 points, which is 3 less than the driver that qualified in 43rd place. All other non-qualifiers earn 3 fewer points than the next fastest non-qualifying time.

After the first 26 races, the top 12 drivers are automatically given 5,000 points, plus an additional 10 points for every first-place finish they have scored. This ensures that only one of the top 12 racers will win the championship. This portion of the season is called the Chase for the Sprint Cup or the Sprint for the Cup.

Richard Childress had Dale Earnhardt's Monte Carlo painted a new color, and Earnhardt's iconic #3 was changed to #29. After a poor qualifying run for his first race, Harvick surprised many NASCAR fans by finishing 14th at the Dura Lube 400 at the North Carolina Speedway in Rockingham. The next weekend at the Las Vegas Motor Speedway in Nevada, Harvick finished 12th in the Busch Series race and eighth in the Winston Series race. Now people truly started paying careful attention to the Winston Cup upstart.

On February 15, 1998, fans and journalists rushed up to Dale Earnhardt's car after he won the Daytona 500. This was Earnhardt's first and only Daytona 500 victory.

An Unexpected Win

Harvick's third Winston Cup race was the Cracker Barrel 500 at the Atlanta Motor Speedway in Georgia. He had come in eighth in the Busch Series race held at the same track the previous day. He qualified fifth and was near the front of the pack for most of the race. After battling Winston Cup stars such as Dale Earnhardt Jr., Jeff Gordon, and Dale Jarrett, Harvick took the lead with just ten laps to go.

On the final lap, Harvick struggled to hold off Jeff Gordon. As they approached the checkered flag, Harvick managed to stay mere inches ahead of Gordon for his first Winston Cup win. He beat Gordon by only 0.006 of a second! This win made Harvick the fifth driver in NASCAR history to come in first in his third start, and the first driver to do it since Dan Gurney in 1963. Many of the drivers he had just defeated showed their good sportsmanship by congratulating Harvick after the race for his remarkable achievement.

Gaining Speed

Harvick's first Winston Cup win was huge news in the sporting world. Television and radio shows swamped him with requests for interviews. But he needed to concentrate on the upcoming races. His hectic schedule often required him to finish a race and then jump on a plane so he could be ready for another race the next day in another city.

Harvick celebrates with his wife, DeLana *(center)*, and crew after winning the Busch Series championship on November 10, 2001. This photo was taken after a race at Miami Speedway in Florida.

Once, he even competed in three races in one weekend, including a Craftsman Truck race.

Harvick won another Winston Cup race in July at Chicagoland Speedway. He finished the season in ninth place with two wins, 16 top-ten finishes, and 4,406 points. In the Busch Series, he had five wins, 20 top-five finishes, 24 top-ten finishes, and 4,813 points. This was good enough to earn him the 2001 Busch Series championship.

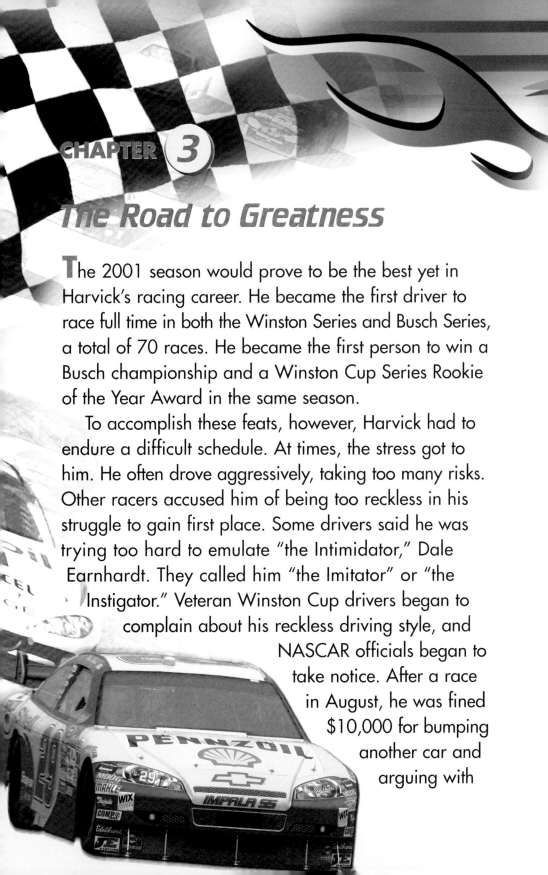

CHAPTER 3

The Road to Greatness

The 2001 season would prove to be the best yet in Harvick's racing career. He became the first driver to race full time in both the Winston Series and Busch Series, a total of 70 races. He became the first person to win a Busch championship and a Winston Cup Series Rookie of the Year Award in the same season.

To accomplish these feats, however, Harvick had to endure a difficult schedule. At times, the stress got to him. He often drove aggressively, taking too many risks. Other racers accused him of being too reckless in his struggle to gain first place. Some drivers said he was trying too hard to emulate "the Intimidator," Dale Earnhardt. They called him "the Imitator" or "the Instigator." Veteran Winston Cup drivers began to complain about his reckless driving style, and NASCAR officials began to take notice. After a race in August, he was fined $10,000 for bumping another car and arguing with

Car owner Richard Childress (left) talks with Kevin Harvick before a test drive at the Indianapolis Motor Speedway on July 25, 2001. Harvick was preparing for the 2001 Brickyard 400.

other drivers, but this did little to slow him down. He nearly got into several fights with other drivers after dangerous developments on the track.

It became apparent to Richard Childress that, despite the stunning rookie season and Busch championship, Harvick was going to need to calm down and stop angering other drivers. However, Harvick wasn't sure he could do this and continue to win.

Nine of the cars involved in the wreck during the 2002 Daytona 500 careen out of control, filling the air with smoke. Harvick's #29 car is at the center of the mayhem.

Disappointment in Daytona

For the 2002 season, Harvick chose to drive part time in the Busch Series and concentrate on winning the Winston Cup. He drove a silver and black Monte Carlo Chevrolet. He had competed in every race in 2001, except for the Daytona 500 in which Dale Earnhardt had died. This would be Harvick's first chance to win in Daytona.

DAYTONA 500: THE GREAT AMERICAN RACE

Racing has long been a tradition in the Florida city of Daytona. Early races there took place on a stretch of highway and an equally long stretch of shoreline. Today, the Daytona International Speedway is home to one of the most exciting opening days in professional sports—the Daytona 500. The Daytona 500 is the first race of every NASCAR season. It is also the race with the largest prize and the most prestige. Many experts believe that a racer has not achieved greatness until winning this race. The 2008 Daytona 500 marked the race's 50th anniversary. Driver Ryan Newman came in first. Kevin Harvick finished in 14th place.

Harvick qualified second and came out racing hard, determined to have another record-breaking season. After holding second place for a portion of the race, driver Jeff Gordon tried to pass Harvick, but Harvick wouldn't budge. The two drivers bumped together and started an 18-car wreck. Harvick wasn't able to finish the race. It was a disappointing beginning to the season.

Sophomore Slump

As the 2002 season progressed, Harvick continued to experience frustration. His racing style continued to draw negative attention from drivers and NASCAR officials. After a Busch Series race at Bristol Motor Speedway, Harvick got into a fight with driver Greg Biffle. NASCAR officials fined Harvick $15,000. Undeterred, Harvick kept racing recklessly and was fined an additional $35,000.

Childress decided to change Harvick's pit crew. That helped settle down the driver, and he improved during the second half of the season. Although he won only one race, his driving became more consistent, and he was able to stay toward the front of the pack for most races. Harvick finished the season in 21st place.

2002 *IROC*

Despite the disappointing results in 2002, Harvick had earned a spot in the 2002 International Race of Champions (IROC). The IROC is an annual series of all-star races. Each year, six to twelve drivers are invited to participate in four races. The driver with the most points at the end of the races is crowned IROC champion of the year. All participants drive the same type of car—a Pontiac Trans Am—prepared by the same team of mechanics. That year, Harvick raced alongside other talented drivers such as Dale Jarrett and Tony Stewart.

Harvick won the 2002 IROC race held in Fontana, California, and had three top-five finishes throughout the IROC series. When the series was over, he walked away with first place overall and $250,000 in winnings. This

Harvick crosses the finish line of a 2002 IROC race, the True Value IROC at the California Speedway in Fontana, California.

victory made Harvick the sixth driver in history to win an IROC title in his first attempt. He competed in the 2003 and 2004 IROC series but was not able to repeat his 2002 victory.

Comeback in 2003

Although Harvick continued to race with all-out determination in 2003, he was more experienced and less reckless. He drove in 19 Busch races and 6 Craftsman Truck races. In the Winston Series, he was reunited with his old Busch Series crew chief, Todd Berrier. Harvick stayed in the top ten throughout the first part of the season.

In what many NASCAR fans and experts consider the biggest win of his career, Harvick notched his first win of the 2003 season at the Brickyard 400 (now called Allstate 400 at the Brickyard). This race is held every year at the Indianapolis Motor Speedway, which is commonly known as the Brickyard because it was originally paved with bricks.

Before most NASCAR races, drivers must qualify. Drivers each take one lap around the course, and they are placed in order based on the quickest qualifying times. While qualifying for the 2003 Brickyard 400, driver Ryan Newman broke a track speed record when he qualified with a speed of 184.238 mph (296.5 km/hr). Harvick quickly reset the record with a speed of 184.343 mph (296.67 km/hr)! Harvick grabbed the pole position for this race, which means he secured the best starting position. Yet, no one had ever won the Brickyard 400 from the pole position.

For most of the race, Harvick battled with other drivers toward the head of the pack. He led for 33 laps during the race. An accident occurred behind the leaders with only 16 laps to go. After restarting the race, Harvick was in second place behind Jamie McMurray. Harvick's teammate Robby Gordon was right behind him blocking other racers—including superstars Jeff Gordon, Matt Kenseth, and Kurt Busch—from passing Harvick. With just ten laps to go, Harvick pulled ahead and held off McMurray for the win. He became the first driver in history to win the Brickyard 400 after starting the race from the pole position.

Although the Brickyard 400 was Harvick's only win in 2003, he had 11 top-five finishes and 18 top-ten finishes. He had his best year ever, ending the season in fifth place with 4,770 points and winning more than $6 million.

Back to Daytona

The next two seasons were filled with problems for Harvick. He finished both in 14th place. Yet, the 2006 season proved to be his best ever. He raced a full Busch Series schedule and dominated the competition. He stunned NASCAR fans with nine wins, 23 top-five finishes, and 32 top-ten finishes. At the end of the season, he was 824 points in front of the nearest driver, Carl Edwards. Harvick easily won his second Busch Cup championship.

He also had great success in the Nextel Cup Series (the former Winston Cup series, renamed for a new corporate sponsor). Despite running full Busch and Nextel schedules, Harvick raced well enough to make it into the 2006 Chase for the Championship. He won the first race of the Chase—the Sylvania 300 at the New Hampshire Motor Speedway in Loudon, New Hampshire. The win gave him the points lead for the first time in his Nextel/ Winston Cup career. He won one more race that year and finished fourth in the standings, his best finish to date. He won a career-high five Nextel Cup races.

Many people had high hopes for Harvick in 2007. He started the season with one of the most exciting Daytona

Harvick celebrates after one of his greatest wins ever—the 2007 Daytona 500. Crewmates, journalists, and fans cheer for Harvick as he stands triumphantly atop his car.

500 victories in NASCAR history. A multicar crash midway through the race knocked out several drivers, including Kurt Busch and Tony Stewart. In the final laps of the race, Mark Martin struggled to stay in front of Kyle Busch. As the pack raced for the finish line, Harvick moved to the outside and shot forward with Matt Kenseth right behind him. He managed to get a few feet ahead of Martin while Busch and Kenseth bumped and spun out of control. Harvick crossed the finish line a mere .02 seconds before Martin. Six years after the tragic death of Dale Earnhardt Sr., Harvick clinched his first Daytona 500 victory.

CHAPTER 4

Beyond the Track

The Daytona 500 was Harvick's only win in 2007, but it was still a great season. He finished in tenth place in the Nextel Series and fourth in the Busch Series. Harvick also won the 2007 Nextel All-Star Challenge. He has continued to be one of NASCAR's greatest competitors, and the #29 Shell-Pennzoil car is a common sight at the front of the pack on most race days. Many fans and experts believe that it's just a matter of time before Harvick joins the ranks of NASCAR's finest drivers as a Sprint Cup champion.

Like many professional NASCAR drivers, Harvick spends much of his time racing or getting ready to race. However, he is more than just a race car driver.

Kevin and DeLana

During the 1999 Busch season, just after Harvick became a member of Richard Childress Racing, he met DeLana Linville.

DeLana Harvick stands with Kevin as he answers questions after the Sylvania 300 on September 17, 2006, at the New Hampshire International Speedway.

DeLana, who is the daughter of former race car driver John Linville, grew up immersed in the sport of racing. She attended races with her father nearly every weekend. Although Linville would have liked to become a driver like father, the valuable racing information she learned watching countless races helped make her a successful NASCAR businesswoman.

Harvick met Linville when she was working as a public relations specialist for driver Randy LaJoie. She had previously worked for driver Jeff Gordon's publicity team. He asked her to go to the Richard Childress Racing holiday party with him, and they became very good friends.

In December 2000, they got engaged. They were married on February 28, 2001, in Las Vegas, Nevada, just before the beginning of Harvick's breakout season. That same weekend, he came in 12th in a Busch Series race and eighth in a Winston Cup race. It was one of the most memorable weeks of his life. Today, Harvick still considers DeLana Linville his best friend.

Kevin Harvick, Inc.

Harvick and Linville loved racing so much that they decided to jump into the ownership end of the business after getting married. He was an up-and-coming NASCAR driver with a great deal of ambition. She was a business-savvy public relations specialist with solid NASCAR experience. Together, they knew they'd make a great team.

The Harvicks founded Kevin Harvick Incorporated (KHI) in 2001. The first KHI vehicle (#33) was a truck built in the garage of Ed Berrier, the brother of Harvick's Winston Cup crew chief Todd Berrier. In 2002, KHI ran six Craftsman Truck races, five with Harvick in the driver's seat. Harvick won his first Craftsman Truck race in November at the Phoenix International Raceway in Arizona. He became the fifth driver in NASCAR history to win a race in all three of NASCAR's most important series (today's Craftsman Truck, Nationwide, and Sprint Cup series). The KHI team finished the season with one win, four top-five finishes, and five top-ten finishes. It was a promising start for the young owners. In 2002, KHI competed in six Craftsman races with Harvick, Ed Berrier, Brandon Miller, and Randy LaJoie driving. Harvick was the best driver of the group, earning one win and three top-five finishes.

In 2004, KHI competed full-time in the Craftsman Truck Series. The #33 truck was sponsored by GM Goodrich and driven by Matt Crafton. The team finished the year sixth in points. KHI also entered two Busch Series races that year. The #77 car was driven by Winston Cup standout Tony Stewart. Stewart's best finish was fifth.

The next season, KHI took a big step forward by competing full-time in both the Craftsman Series and the Busch Series. Driver Ron Hornaday drove the #33 truck for most of the races KHI competed in. Hornaday finished fifth in the points standings at the end of the season, which was the best finish yet for a KHI driver. In the Busch Series, Tony Stewart drove the #33 car and won KHI's first Busch race on opening day— February 19, 2005—at the Daytona International Speedway. Driver Tony Raines drove the #77 car for most of the races that season. The #33 team finished the Busch season with one win, five top-five finishes, and 13 top-ten finishes. The #33 team also finished tenth in the owners' point standings. Hornaday led the #33 Craftsman Truck team to a seventh place finish in 2005.

In 2006, KHI expanded again by adding another full-time Busch Series car—the #77 car driven by rookie Burney Lamar. Tony Stewart repeated his opening-day victory in the #33 car. The #33 car finished the year tenth in the points standing, and the #77 car finished in 24th.

Hornaday was determined to win a Craftsman Truck title in 2007. With Camping World sponsoring the #33 car, Hornaday had his best season to date. Toward the end of the season, he was in close contention for the championship with driver Mike Skinner. During the last race of the year, Skinner had trouble with his tires, which allowed Hornaday to pass him in the points race. Hornaday finished the season with 3,982 points and the Craftsman Truck championship. Not only was this Hornaday's first championship, it was the first championship for KHI as well. Hornaday and KHI were hoping to repeat this accomplishment in 2008.

KHI might have started as a tiny operation in a friend's garage, but it has come a long way in just a few years. Today, KHI headquarters in Kernersville, North Carolina, is a modern 70,000-square-foot (6,503 sq. m) facility housing two full-time Nationwide Series teams and two full-time Craftsman Truck Series teams. It may not be very long before KHI branches out into the Sprint Cup Series.

Harvick on Health and Drug Use

Ever since he was a wrestler in high school, Harvick has understood the importance of exercise, eating right, and avoiding harmful drugs. Recently, he and other drivers have spoken out about the lack of drug testing in NASCAR. For years, the NASCAR policy on drug testing has been to conduct a drug test only in the case of reasonable suspicion.

For some concerned drivers, however, this is not enough. In an article posted on ESPN.com, Harvick said: "In the ten years that I've raced, I've never been drug-tested. To me, that's not a proper drug policy for a professional sport. We haven't made any headway whatsoever on the drug-testing policy."

After discussions among prominent NASCAR personalities about the use of drugs, Harvick was perhaps the most vocal proponent of regular drug testing in NASCAR. In fact, he quickly set a positive example by implementing a drug testing policy within KHI. All of his employees have been tested, and Harvick hopes that other owners will soon follow his lead.

Spare Time

What does a superstar NASCAR driver do in his spare time? When it comes to Harvick, the answer is . . . race cars, of course! He has an asphalt go-kart track at his home in North Carolina. The track comes complete with bleachers and lighting. Racing go-karts every weekend is his way of relaxing. He and several other drivers, including Tony Stewart and Clint Bowyer, have friendly yet competitive races on Harvick's track whenever they find the time. They even made a trophy for the winner of each race. Aside from racing go-karts, Harvick enjoys remote-control cars, all-terrain vehicles (ATVs), video games, and skeet shooting.

The Future

In 2008, Harvick continued to excel as a professional NASCAR driver and car owner. He is a common sight at the head of the pack during most races. He continues to

A CHARITABLE DRIVER

Kevin and DeLana Harvick are constantly taking care of KHI and preparing for Kevin's next race, but they still manage to find time to help others. On his Web site, KevinHarvick.com, Harvick relates that he is very happy to autograph pictures and collectibles for fans, especially when they are used for charity events.

Harvick is also a proud contributor to the Victory Junction Gang Camp. Driver Kyle Petty and his wife, Pattie, started the camp in honor of their son Adam, who died in 1999 in a racing accident. Patterned on and affiliated with the Hole in the Wall Gang camps founded by actor Paul Newman, Victory Junction Gang is a year-round camp for children with health issues that would normally keep them from attending sleepaway camps. Donations from individuals and corporations keep the camp running. Many NASCAR drivers, including Harvick, are active and vocal supporters of Victory Junction Gang. KHI is one of the camp's corporate sponsors. In addition to donating money, KHI sponsors, hosts, and participates in numerous functions each year to raise funds for the camp.

On August 10, 2002, Harvick relaxes before the Sirius Satellite 400 at Watkins Glen International Raceway by playing with his radio-controlled truck—truck #29, of course!

race with the pedal to the metal, but experience and knowledge have helped him to create a successful and professional racing style. His Craftsman Truck KHI teams are hoping for a repeat of 2007's championship. At the time of this writing, Harvick himself had won more than $36 million in Sprint Cup races alone (a total that includes his Winston and Nextel Cup series earnings) and was a two-time Busch/Nationwide Series champion. When will Harvick win the Sprint Cup championship? It seems almost certain that it will just be a matter of time.

Glossary

asphalt A material used for surfacing roads.

dominate To exert a strong influence over someone or something; to completely control.

emulate To greatly admire someone and seek to model one's behavior after that person.

enthusiast Someone who is passionate about something, such as a sport or hobby.

exhibition A public demonstration.

instigate To cause trouble.

intimidate To frighten someone into doing something or not doing something.

modified Changed from an original state.

pole position The best position on the starting grid of a car race, usually given to the driver with the fastest prerace lap time.

prestige Displaying obvious importance.

proponent Someone who is an advocate for or strongly supports something, such as a cause.

public relations specialist A person who is responsible for establishing, maintaining, and improving the relationship between an institution or person and the public.

qualify To earn the right to move on to a next stage.

sanction Official permission from a governing body.

skeet shooting A form of sport shooting where clay disks are fired into the air at speeds and angles intended to simulate the flight of birds.

sponsor A person or business that provides money in return for advertising.

stock car A standard automobile that has been modified for professional racing.

suspicion The unproven belief that something is wrong.

tutelage Instruction and guidance provided by someone more experienced.

unanimous Agreed on by everyone concerned.

For More Information

Kevin Harvick Fan Club
P.O. Box 1491
West Monroe, LA 71294
Web site: http://www.kevinharvick.com/fanclub.htm
The official fan club of NASCAR racer Kevin Harvick.

Kevin Harvick Incorporated (KHI)
703 Park Lawn Court
Kernersville, NC 27284
Web site: http://www.kevinharvickinc.com
The official site of KHI, the parent company of Kevin Harvick's NASCAR
    racing teams.

The NASCAR Foundation
One Wachovia Center
301 South College Street, Suite 3900
Charlotte, NC 28202
Web site: http://foundation.nascar.com
The NASCAR Foundation supports a wide range of charitable initiatives
    that reflect the core values of the entire NASCAR family. The
    foundation uses the strength of the sport and its people to make
    a difference in the lives of those who need it most.

National Association for Stock Car Auto Racing (NASCAR)
P.O. Box 2875
Daytona Beach, FL 32120
(386) 253-0611
Web site: http://www.nascar.com
NASCAR, which celebrated 60 years in 2008, is the sanctioning body
    for one of North America's premier sports. NASCAR is the number
    one spectator sport in the United States and is the number two–
    rated regular season sport on television.

For More Information

Richard Childress Racing (RCR)
425 Industrial Drive
Welcome, NC 27374
(336) 731-3334, ext. 3466
Web site: http://www.rcrracing.com
RCR has earned nearly 180 victories and 11 NASCAR championships, including the 2007 NASCAR Nationwide Series owners' point title and six championships in the Cup series with the legendary Dale Earnhardt Sr. RCR was the first organization to win championships in the Sprint Cup Series, Nationwide Series, and Craftsman Truck Series.

Victory Junction Gang Camp
4500 Adam's Way
Randleman, NC 27317
(877) VJG-CAMP (854-2267)
Web site: http://www.victoryjunction.org
The Victory Junction Gang Camp is a year-round camp that enriches the lives of children ages 7 to 15 who have chronic medical conditions or serious illnesses. The camp provides life-changing camping experiences that are exciting, fun, and empowering, in a safe and medically sound environment. The camp was founded by Kyle and Pattie Petty, in honor of their son Adam. Victory Junction Gang Camp has a racing theme with the sights, sounds, look, and feel of a racetrack.

Web Sites

Due to the changing nature of Internet links, Rosen Publishing has developed an online list of Web sites related to the subject of this book. This site is updated regularly. Please use this link to access this list:

http://www.rosenlinks.com/bw/keha

For Further Reading

Burt, William. *NASCAR's Best: Top Drivers Past and Present*. Osceola, WI: Motorbooks, 2004.

Dallenbach, Robin, and Anita Rich. *Portraits of NASCAR*. Marietta, GA: Motorsports Family LLC, 2008.

Fielden, Greg. *NASCAR: The Complete History*. New York, NY: Publications International, 2007.

Hester, Elizabeth, ed. *NASCAR*. New York, NY: DK Publishing, 2005.

Lazarus, William P. *The Sands of Time: A Century of Racing in Daytona Beach*. Champaign, IL: Sports Publishing, LLC, 2004.

Martin, Mark, and Beth Tuschak. *NASCAR for Dummies*. Hoboken, NJ: Wiley, 2005.

Stewart, Mark, and Mike Kennedy. *NASCAR at the Track*. Minneapolis, MN: Lerner Publications Company, 2008.

Stewart, Mark, and Mike Kennedy. *NASCAR Designed to Win*. Minneapolis, MN: Lerner Publications Company, 2008.

Bibliography

Black Book Partners. "Kevin Harvick Bio." JockBio.com. Retrieved April 27, 2008 (http://www.jockbio.com/Bios/Harvick_Kevin/Harvick_bio.html).

Blount, Terry. "Harvick, Stewart, JJ, Kahne Say They've Never Been Drug Tested." ESPN.com, April 1, 2008. Retrieved April 28, 2008 (http://sports.espn.go.com/rpm/nascar/cup/news/story?id=3340113).

Burt, William. *Behind the Scenes of NASCAR Racing*. St. Paul, MN: Motorbooks International, 2003.

Dunn, Jeremy. "Kevin Harvick Biography." Suite101.com, October 11, 2007. Retrieved April 27, 2008 (http://nascar.suite101.com/article.cfm/kevin_harvick_biography).

Fleischman, Bill, and Al Pearce. *The Unauthorized NASCAR Fan Guide 2004*. Canton, MI: Visible Ink Press, 2004.

Golenbock, Peter, and Greg Fielden, eds. *NASCAR Encyclopedia*. St. Paul, MN: Motorbooks International, 2003.

Harvick, Kevin. "Kevin's Diary Entry: Martinsville Race Weekend." KevinHarvick.com. Retrieved April 28, 2008 (http://www.kevinharvick.com/Diaries/martinsville.htm).

KevinHarvick.com. "DeLana Harvick." Retrieved April 28, 2008 (http://www.kevinharvickinc.com/Teams/DHarvick.htm).

KevinHarvick.com. "The History of KHI." Retrieved April 28, 2008 (http://www.kevinharvickinc.com/history.htm).

KevinHarvick.com. "Kevin Harvick: Driven to Win." Retrieved April 27, 2008 (http://www.kevinharvick.com/biography1.htm).

Long, Dustin. "Kevin Harvick: In His Own Words." *Roanoke Times*, March 29, 2008. Retrieved April 15, 2008 (http://www.roanoke.com/sports/racing/wb/156260).

Martin, Bruce. "Far from Satisfied." SportsIllustrated.com, February 8, 2008. Retrieved April 27, 2008 (http://sportsillustrated.cnn.com/2008/writers/bruce_martin/02/08/kevin.harvick/index.html).

Miller, Timothy, and Steve Milton. *NASCAR Now!* Buffalo, NY: Firefly Books, 2006.

KEVIN HARVICK: NASCAR Driver

NASCAR.com. "NASCAR Points System and Chase." Retrieved April 21, 2008 (http://www.nascar.com/guides/about/points/index.html).

Racing-reference.info. "Kevin Harvick (driver)." Retrieved April 27, 2008 (http://www.racing-reference.info/driver?id=harvike01).

Racing-reference.info. "Kevin Harvick (owner)." Retrieved April 28, 2008 (http://www.racing-reference.info/owner?id=harvike01).

SceneDaily.com. "Harvick Institutes Substance-Abuse Policy for Team He Owns." April 26, 2008. Retrieved April 28, 2003 (http://www.kevinharvickinc.com/2008News/042508a.htm).

SportsIllustrated.com. "'An Awesome Lap': Harvick Sets Track Record in Winning Brickyard Pole." August 2, 2003. Retrieved April 27, 2008 (http://sportsillustrated.cnn.com/motorsports/2003/brickyard400/news/2003/08/02/brickyard_qual_ap/).

SportsIllustrated.com. "Goin' Yard: Pole Sitter Harvick Cruises to First Brickyard 400 Win." August 4, 2003. Retrieved April 27, 2008 (http://sportsillustrated.cnn.com/motorsports/2003/brickyard400/news/2003/08/03/brickyard_400_ap/).

Index

About the Author

Greg Roza writes and edits educational materials. He has a master's degree in English from the State University of New York at Fredonia. He enjoys athletic activities in his spare time and loves watching NASCAR on television. Roza lives in Hamburg, New York, with his wife, Abigail, and their three children—Autumn, Lincoln, and Daisy.

Photo Credits

Cover Darrell Ingham/Getty Images; pp. 1, 4, 7, 14, 23, 32 Doug Pensinger/Getty Images; p. 6 aiwirepix/Newscom; pp. 9, 17, 22 upiphotos/Newscom; p. 11 Robert Laberge/Getty Images; pp. 15, 25, 40 © AP Images; p. 20 © Jim Gund/Icon SMI; p. 24 krtphotos/Newscom; p. 28 Kevin Kane/WireImage/Getty Images; p. 31 Jonathan Ferrey/Getty Images; p. 33 Rusty Jarrett/Getty Images.

Designer: Evelyn Horovicz; Photo Researcher: Amy Feinberg

DATE DUE

SEP 0 0

Please do not remove this card from pocket

GAYLORD 143

Please do not remove this card from pocket